DOGS

MICHAELA MILLER

Contents

Words in bold, **like this**, are explained in the glossary on page 23.

Wild ones

Dogs can be as big as a great Dane or as small as a chihuahua. But no matter how big or small, all dogs are related to wolves.

great Dane

Wolves were probably first kept as pets about 12,000 years ago. They were used to guard and protect their owners.

wolf

Dogs can live for between ten and eighteen years.

The dog for you

Dogs and puppies are lots of fun, but they also need a lot of looking after. If you and your family really want a dog, talk it over carefully for a long time.

DOG FACT

Around the world, more than 200 million dogs are kept as pets.

Ask a vet for advice about the right type of dog for you. Big dogs are not a good idea in a house with young children. Big, strong dogs can easily push small children over.

5

Where to find your dog

Start looking for a dog at your local RSPCA **animal shelter**. The people who work there should ask you all sorts of questions. They should also visit your house to make sure you get the right dog for your home.

dog at an animal shelter

6

golden retriever puppies

If you want a special kind of puppy, a **pedigree** one, you need to get it from a **breeder**. This is a person who sells dogs. The vet may know some good breeders.

Dogs need exercise and lots of company – otherwise they will be unhappy.

Healthy dogs and puppies

Healthy dogs and puppies have a soft, clean, shiny coat and skin without any lumps, cuts or rashes. Their eyes are bright and clear. Their ears are soft and pink inside. They should have a moist, cold nose and a clean bottom.

a healthy dog

DOG FACT

Dogs need exercise and lots of company – otherwise they will be unhappy.

A happy dog or puppy will be pleased to see you.

9

Feeding time

Ask the vet for advice about food. Big dogs need more food than small ones. Adult dogs need one or two meals a day. Puppies need three or four. Dogs and puppies must always have a bowl of fresh water.

You can buy dog food at supermarkets and pet shops. Follow the instructions on the packet or tin carefully. Most dogs need a mixture of **cereal** and tinned food.

DOG FACT

If you feed a dog or puppy too much, it will become fat and unhealthy.

Home sweet home

Dogs and puppies need a bed of their own. A chew-proof plastic basket with a washable mattress is a good idea. Some dogs like washable beanbags too. Put the bed in a quiet spot away from draughts.

Dogs like toys, especially ones they can chew. Make sure the toys are strong, and not too small or your dog might swallow them.

Your dog will need a brush and maybe a comb of its own. Ask the vet which is the right sort for its coat.

13

Stepping out

Dogs need to be exercised at least once a day. The vet can tell you about training and exercising your dog. Ask the vet what sort of collar and lead you should buy.

All puppies and dogs need proper training. They must be trained to walk without pulling anyone over. They should come when they are called and sit when they are told to.

Dogs' mess can carry diseases. Always clean up after your dog.

Keeping clean

Make sure that your dog's food and water bowls are washed well after every meal. Its bed must also be kept clean.

a dog in a plastic basket

Cats can get worms which live in their stomachs and make them sick. Take your cat to the veterinarian if it has worms.

You will need to check your cat for fleas. Fleas can live on the cat, bite it, and make its skin itchy. If your cat has fleas, the veterinarian can suggest something to get rid of them.

At the Veterinarian

Besides you, a veterinarian is your cat's best friend. When you get your new cat take it to the veterinarian for a checkup. The veterinarian will say when your cat should have **shots** to stop it catching diseases.

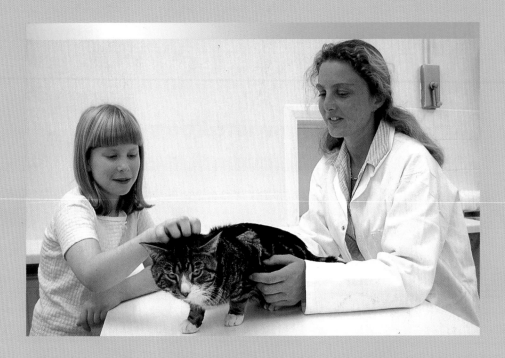

These shots are usually done once a year with a regular checkup and are very important. They could save your cat's life and also stop diseases spreading to other cats and kittens.

To find the name of a local veterinarian, look in the Yellow Pages or ask friends who have pets.

No More Kittens

There are many unwanted cats and kittens in the world and not enough people to take care of them. Don't let your cat—male or female—add to the problem. Your veterinarian can tell you how **neutering** will help.

CAT FACT

A female cat that has not been neutered can have up to three litters of kittens a year, with five kittens in each litter.

mother feeding her young

Lots of owners find that their male cats are much easier to live with when they have been neutered. It stops them wandering off and fighting. Female cats will not have kittens if they have been neutered.

21

A Note From the ASPCA

Pets are often our good friends for the very best of reasons. They don't care how we look, how we dress, or who our friends are. They like us because we are nice to them and take care of them. That's what being friends is all about.

This book has given you information to help you know what your pet needs. Learn all you can from this book and others, and from people who know about animals, such as veterinarians and workers at animal shelters like the ASPCA. You will soon become your pet's most important friend.

More Books to Read

Fowler, Allan. *It Could Still be a Cat.* Columbus Ohio: Childrens Press, 1993.

Kalman, Bobbie and Tammie Events. *Little Cats.* New York: Crabtree Publishing Co., 1994.

Glossary

When words in this book are in bold, **like this,** they are explained in this glossary.

animal shelters There are many of these shelters all around the country that look after unwanted pets and try to find them new homes.

grooming This means brushing and combing your cat.

litter box This is a box where a cat can go to the bathroom. It can be filled with soil or with special material called litter.

neutering This is an operation to stop cats being able to have kittens.

shots Cats have to have shots from a veterinarian to stop them catching diseases.

vitamins and minerals Most foods contain vitamins and minerals. A good diet will have enough of the right vitamins and minerals to keep an animal healthy.

Index

Published by Heinemann Interactive Library, an imprint of Reed Educational & Professional Publishing,
1350 East Touhy Avenue, Suite 240 West, Des Plaines, IL 60018

Produced by Times Offset (M) Sdn. Bhd.
Designed by Nicki Wise and Lisa Nutt
Illustrations by Michael Strand

02 01 00 99 98
10 9 8 7 6 5 4 3 2 1

Library of Congress Cataloging-in-Publication Data
Miller, Michaela, 1961-
   Cats / Michaela Miller.
   p. cm. — (Pets)
   Includes bibliographical reference and index.
   Summary: A simple introduction to choosing and caring for a cat.
   ISBN 1-57572-572-X (lib. bdg.)
   1. Cats — Juvenile literature. [1. Cats. 2. Pets.] 1. Title.
II. Series: Miller, Michaela. 1961- Pets.
SF445.7.M55 1998   97-16614
636.8'083—dc21   CIP
                                                            AC

Acknowledgments
The author and publishers are grateful to the following for permission to reproduce copyright photographs.
Dave Bradford pp3, 5, 8-15, 17; Bruce Coleman Ltd/ p21 Jane Burton; RSPCA/ p2 Julie Meech,
p6 Colin Seddon, pp4, 7 E A Janes, pp16, 20 Angela Hampton, pp18, 19 Tim Sambrook.
Cover photographs reproduced with permission of: RSPCA; Dave Bradford
With special thanks to the ASPCA and their consultant Dr. Stephen Zawistowski, who approved the contents of this book.
Every effort has been made to contact copyright holders of any material reproduced in this book.
Any omissions will be rectified in subsequent printings if notice is given to the publisher.

24